Trav

CAN YOU SURVIVE A
SUPERVOLCANO
ERUPTION?

...nsday Adventure

by BLAKE HOENA

illustrated by FILIPPO VANZO

CAPSTONE PRESS
a capstone imprint

You Choose Books are published by Capstone Press,
1710 Roe Crest Drive, North Mankato, Minnesota 56003
www.mycapstone.com

Library of Congress Cataloging-in-Publication Data
Cataloging-in-publication information is on file with the Library of Congress.
ISBN 978-1-4914-8108-0 (hardcover
ISBN 978-1-4914-8126-4 (paperback)
ISBN 978-1-4914-8132-5 (eBook PDF)

Editorial Credits
Mari Bolte, editor; Bobbie Nuytten, designer;
Jo Miller, media researcher; Gene Bentdahl,
production specialist; Nathan Gassman, creative director

Photo Credits
Shutterstock: Andrejs Zavadskis, (background, throughout), Galyna Andrushko,
102, photka, 108

Printed in US.
009742R

TABLE OF CONTENTS

ABOUT YOUR
ADVENTURE

YOU are living through a major national disaster—a supervolcano. It's up to you to make the right choices. Will you live to see another day? Or will you be one of the many buried in the supervolcano's ash? Start by turning the page. Then follow the directions at the bottom of each page. The choices you make will change the outcome. After you finish one path, go back and read the others to see how the decisions you make change your fate. Do you have what it takes to survive a supervolcano?

YOU CHOOSE the path you take through a supervolcano eruption.

KA-BOOM!

"We're here!" your friend Terry exclaims. "We're finally here!"

You and Terry press your faces to the dusty windows of the tour bus. Tall pines line the road. Snow-capped mountains rise up all around you. Crystal blue lakes dot the landscape. You've been waiting for months to see Yellowstone National Park.

"What do you want to see first?" Terry asks. "Old Faithful? The Sulphur Spring?"

"Don't forget about the Mud Volcano," you say.

The mountains fall away as the bus rumbles down into a large, rolling plateau. This area is what makes the park so unique. It is filled with hot springs, bubbling mud pots, and hundreds of steaming geysers. Mr. Thwaites, your science teacher, told you Yellowstone has more geothermal features than any other place on Earth.

Turn the page.

With perfect timing, Mr. Thwaites stands up at the front of the bus. Not only is he the trip leader, he also taught a special class about the park before you left.

"OK, everyone, listen up," he, says. "We are now entering the Yellowstone Caldera."

You learned this huge crater was created when a supervolcano erupted here more than 600,000 years ago. The caldera is about 40 miles wide, and just a few miles under your feet, sits a huge magma lake. Heat rising up from the molten rock is what causes all the geysers and hot springs in the park.

"We're almost to where we will be staying," Mr. Thwaites continues. "When you get off the bus, you'll meet the research assistant who you have been assigned to work with."

Even though you're excited to be here instead of sitting at school, you know this trip won't be all about having fun. Sure, you'll get to hike around and see many of the park's sights. But you chose Yellowstone National Park over other possible destinations because you thought it'd be interesting to learn about the area's geological features. You and your classmates will be staying here for a couple weeks as you study the park. Then you'll put together a final project to present when you get back to school.

Turn the page.

Your bus pulls up to a group of small, rustic cabins that you'll call home during your stay. They don't have electricity, running water, or Internet. "It'll be an experience," you tell yourself as you pocket your phone.

A group of college-age students wait outside the bus. They are all dressed in dusty jeans and hiking boots, and each holds up a card with a different name. You walk up to the woman who has your name.

"Hi," you say.

"Hey, I'm Isabella," she says with a smile. "But call me Izzy. Everyone else does."

"OK, sure," you reply as you shake her hand.

"This way," she says. "I'll be showing you around the park, and you'll be helping me out." She winks. "I'll make sure you go back to school with a good project."

"Hey! Last one to the cabin gets bottom bunk!" Terry calls.

Izzy grins and says, "Why don't you go check out your cabin and get some rest? Our days start early around here."

You dash into the cabin, but you're too late. "Dibs!" Terry says from the top bunk.

The rest of the day, you and your classmates simply settle in. It's been a long trip to get to the park, and you're exhausted. Izzy stops by and asks you to think about what kind of research you want to do.

To research the seismic activity in the park,
turn to page 12.
To research the gases and geysers in the park,
turn to page 17.

You decide to help Izzy study the park's seismic activity. You spend the first couple days testing monitors set up around Yellowstone. These monitors measure vibrations in the ground and send their readings to the Yellowstone Volcano Observatory. You spend a lot of time driving and hiking around the park, which makes the work extra enjoyable.

One afternoon in the field, you feel the earth beneath you shake. You stop in your tracks, afraid the ground is going to crumble away under your feet.

"What was that?" you ask.

"Just an earthquake," Izzy says, not looking up from her work.

"*Just* an earthquake?" you ask, your voice squeaking in fear.

"Yeah, we have hundreds around here every year," Izzy explains. "Most are small and register less than 2.0 on the Richter scale. The park's seismic monitors pick them up, but most people don't notice them."

Turn the page.

"But I felt that one," you counter.

"That one must have been at least a 3," Izzy says. "Those are pretty rare."

Later that afternoon, Izzy logs into the Yellowstone Volcano Observatory site to check the park's seismic readings. The earthquake you felt registered 3.2 on the Richter scale. It wasn't strong enough to cause any damage, but several tourists around the park reported it.

The next morning you are shaken awake. But it's not Terry who's trying to wake you. The bed is shaking. The windows are rattling in their frames. The walls of your small cabin sound like they are about to fall apart. By time you realize what's happening, the shaking stops.

Terry, from the top bunk, looks down at you.

"That must have been a 5," Terry says. "Maybe even a 6!"

The park hasn't had an earthquake that strong in years. You're excited to see the seismic readings on Izzy's computer. You jump from bed and get dressed before darting out the door.

Even though it's still dark out, you are pretty familiar with this part of the park. You and Terry quickly find Izzy's cabin. When you get there, you're surprised to see the other research assistants milling around outside.

"That was at least a 6," one of them exclaims.

"See?" says Terry, elbowing you.

"I've been trying to reach the Yellowstone Volcano Observatory," another complains, "but I haven't been able to get a good connection."

"Well, let's gather as much data as we can," Izzy says.

Turn the page.

Brad, the research assistant working with Terry, asks, "Should we check the seismic activity or the surface deformation measurements?"

"What's that?" you whisper to Terry.

"It's the movement of the ground," Terry explains. "It's one way to tell if the magma below us is moving. Let's see if we can help."

To check the park's seismic activity, turn to page 21.
To check the park's ground movement, turn to page 27.

You've been at the park almost a week now. Mostly, you follow Izzy around as she observes different features of the park. You help her take water samples from the hot springs, check the temperature in the mud pits, and record the eruption of geysers. It's hard work and you are constantly busy. But it also allows you to see parts of the park that most visitors never get a chance to see.

One day Izzy receives a call as you're working. You hear her say, "We'll look into it," before hanging up.

"What's up?" you ask.

"Some hikers reported a stand of dead pine trees along the Otter River," she says. "We need to check it out."

You and Izzy hop into a truck and head toward the northeastern corner of the caldera, near the Otter River. You get out and hike a few miles along its bank.

Turn the page.

Sure enough, you spot a stand of pines that have turned brown. You touch one branch, and the needles fall to the ground.

"What could cause this?" you ask.

"I'm not sure," Izzy says.

She radios in your findings.

"Check out the CO_2 levels," you hear the staticky voice on the other end of the radio say.

Izzy looks puzzled.

"What's wrong?" you ask.

"I don't want to frighten you," she says as she digs through her backpack. She finds what she's looking for—a palm-sized monitor—and looks you in the eye. "Sometimes … volcanoes will vent CO_2 gases before they erupt."

Suddenly, your heart starts to race. You're standing in one of the world's largest active volcanoes, with a lake of magma just miles beneath you.

Turn the page.

"Are we in danger?" you ask.

"I doubt there's anything to worry about," Izzy says, shaking her head. " Yellowstone has been dormant for thousands of years."

You're not sure you completely believe her, but you have a task to do. You follow Izzy while she waves the monitor around. As numbers flash on its small screen, she calls them out to you to record. After a while, she stops.

"The CO_2 levels in this area are elevated," she says quietly. She solemnly radios in her findings as you walk back to the truck. "What do you want to do?" she asks.

To stay at the park, turn to page 25.
To leave the park, turn to page 31.

You, Izzy, Brad, and Terry get set up in Izzy's cabin. While Izzy boots up her computer, Brad uses his smartphone to set up a hotspot. With a little maneuvering, they are able to get onto the Yellowstone Volcano Observatory site and check out the seismic activity in the park. Bouncing lines fill the screen.

"Look," Terry says. "It was a 6.1. You were right."

"Should we be worried?" you ask as a small aftershock rattles the cabin.

The fact that neither Brad nor Izzy answer right away does nothing to make you feel better.

Then Brad says, "Something's not right."

"Is that a harmonic tremor?" Izzy asks, fear in her voice.

"What does that mean?" you ask as you peek at the monitor. All the lines mean nothing to you.

"It means the magma under the park is moving," Brad says, his eyes glued to the monitor.

Turn the page.

"And that's bad?" Terry asks.

Izzy can't meet your eyes. "It could create a vent."

"You mean … a volcano," you say.

"You two should get back to your group," Izzy says, snapping the laptop shut. "Park officials might want to evacuate the park if this continues."

You start to argue, but you can see by the stern look Izzy gives you that it's best to listen.

You and Terry head back toward your cabin. On the way, you see Mr. Thwaites. He's been going cabin to cabin checking on the students

"We've been ordered to evacuate," he says. "Our bus will be here in about 30 minutes. You should pack up quick."

Turn the page.

A half an hour later, you're climbing onto the bus. Mr. Thwaites is in the front seat and talking to the bus driver.

"We came through the south exit," the bus driver says. "Traffic is going to be heavy that way, though. We could go out the north exit instead."

"But the north exit will take us quite a ways out of our way," Mr. Thwaites argues.

To leave through the south exit, turn to page 44.
To leave from the north exit, turn to page 47.

You head back to the cabins. That afternoon, Mr. Thwaites gathers all of your classmates together.

"Park officials have put a voluntary evacuation order in place," he explains. "They noticed some CO_2 venting from the ground, which is a warning sign of an eruption. But any volcanic activity is highly unlikely. I just need to make sure that you are aware of any potential dangers."

As your teacher talks, Terry turns to you and says, "Can you believe this? We've only been here a few days, and we might have to leave."

Looking around, you can tell most of your classmates feel the same way. Disappointed groans and mumbles fill the air.

"Now, you don't have to leave," Mr. Thwaites says. "But whether you stay is a decision that needs to be made between you and your parents."

Turn the page.

You text your parents right away. *Nothing to worry about. I'm fine and want to stay.*

We trust you, your mom texts back.

We miss you, your dad adds.

See you when I get back, you text back.

A couple of your classmates are packing up to go, but you and Terry have permission to stay. The threat of an eruption is extremely rare. The voluntary evacuation is just a precaution.

The next morning, you are back in the field. You and Izzy tag along with Terry and his research assistant, Brad, to check the monitors that measure the movement of the ground around the park. A couple of the monitors have been picking up some odd readings. They report that the ground has risen several feet.

The first monitor you check is not far from a stand of dead pines. Terry and Brad hike off to look at another monitor a few miles down the road.

As Izzy bends over the small disc-shaped object, the ground shakes violently. You grab onto a tree to keep your balance.

A loud roar grabs your attention. It sounds somewhat like the sound of a jet airplane flying overhead. You look up to see a plume of ash and smoke shooting skyward in the distance.

Seconds later, Izzy's radio crackles to life. "Um, hello, is someone there?" It's Terry. "We need help. Can you come pick us up?"

You can hear Brad moaning in the background.

"We're on our way," Izzy shouts into the radio.

Turn the page.

You hop into the truck, and then Izzy speeds off. Brad and Terry didn't get very far before the earthquake hit. You see Terry waving you down from the side of the road.

"What happened?" you ask

"He fell when the earthquake hit," Terry says.

"I hit a rock," Brad adds. "I think I broke something."

You and Terry help him into the truck. Then Izzy drives you all to the hospital. On the way, you stare out the back window. You can see the stream of ash behind you.

"Is that a volcano?" you ask.

Turn the page.

"Yeah, it's a vent," Brad says. "But from the look of it, just a small one."

"And it's pretty far from us," Izzy adds. "As long as more vents don't open up, there shouldn't be much to worry about."

You aren't so sure. The cloud of ash piling upward looks dark and ominous.

To stay at the hospital, turn to page 33.
To head back to your group, turn to page 37.

That afternoon, Mr. Thwaites gathers all of your classmates together. You already think you know what he's going to say, though. You saw the tour bus on the way to the meeting.

"OK, everyone, listen up," he starts. "Park officials have requested a voluntary evacuation. And—" He is interrupted by loud groans of disbelief.

"I know, I know you're disappointed. But I've spoken with school officials," he continues. "They have decided it's best if we leave the park."

You can't believe it. You've waited months to get here, and your trip isn't even half over. Now you have to leave.

"But no one thinks there'll be an eruption," Terry objects. "Brad said it was probably nothing." You nod in agreement. Even after the news of the CO_2 gas, Izzy said that an eruption here was highly unlikely.

Turn the page.

"This is out of my hands," Mr. Thwaites says firmly. "Now I need everyone to pack up, and we'll meet by the tour bus in an hour."

You and Terry walk back to your cabin. No one is happy about what is happening, and you hear plenty of grumbling from your classmates.

An hour later, you get onto the tour bus. Mr. Thwaites is talking to the bus driver.

"We aren't the only ones leaving today," the bus driver says. "So the south entrance is pretty backed up with traffic."

"Is there a better exit to take?" Mr. Thwaites asks.

To leave through the east exit, turn to page 51.
To leave through the west exit, turn to page 54.

You and Izzy help Brad out of the truck and into the park's hospital. Terry ran ahead to find him a wheelchair but came back empty-handed. When you get into the hospital, you understand why.

Between the earlier earthquake and this afternoon's eruption, the hospital has filled up with tourists who have suffered an assortment of bruises and broken bones. The place is in complete chaos.

"What's going on?" you ask a passing nurse.

"We're under a mandatory evacuation order because of the eruption," the nurse says. "But people keep coming in, which is making it hard for us to get the patients who are already here ready to go."

Turn the page.

Soon you see buses rolling up to the hospital. You, Terry, and Izzy help injured patients. A nurse looks at Brad's leg before you put him onto a bus too.

Once Brad is safely on board, Izzy says, "We should get you back to your group. Mr. Thwaites is probably looking all over for you."

Turn the page.

She drives you back to the cabins. The area is surprisingly quiet. You don't see any of your classmates around.

"Where is everyone?" Terry asks.

"They must have left already," you say, unsure.

"Well, pack up your things," Izzy says. She tries to sound confident. "We'll try to catch up with them."

As you're packing, the ground shakes. Izzy rushes into your cabin. "Get down! Get down!" she shouts. "There's been another eruption!" You can barely hear her over the deafening roar that follows.

You, Terry, and Izzy duck under your bed to hide. But it doesn't matter. A cloud of burning ash and gas sweeps overhead. Everything it touches—including your cabin—is instantly incinerated.

THE END
To follow another path, turn to page 10.
To learn more about supervolcanoes, turn to page 103.

As Izzy disappears into the hospital with Brad, you look at Terry. "We should get back to our group," you suggest.

Walking seems like the fastest way back. Your cabins are only a few miles away. On the way, you and Terry talk about what has happened. After the recent eruption, you doubt your group will be allowed to stay in the park. There is probably already a mandatory evacuation in effect.

Suddenly, you hear a roar like a locomotive. The earth quakes, and you nearly fall to the ground.

"Look!" Terry shouts once you regain your balance. He points off in the distance.

You turn to see a second plume of fiery ash streaming into the sky. Only this vent is larger than the first, and closer.

"We need to get out of here," you shout.

"How?" Terry asks.

To follow the road to an exit, turn to page 38.
To keep walking toward the cabins, turn to page 41.

You decide that following the road until you find an exit is the best plan. As you make your way, you hear a man shout, "Need a lift?"

You turn to see a pickup truck screech to a stop beside you. You and Terry run around to the passenger side.

"Squeeze in back," a woman in the front passenger seat says. You're barely buckled in when the man speeds off.

"We need to hurry, Frank," the woman says to the man. Frank looks up in the rearview window, and his look of concern is reflected back at you. You look out the back window. What you see horrifies you. A cloud of fiery ash is looming larger and larger, and it's not just shooting upward. It's also spreading out along the ground like a gray tidal wave. The cloud of ash is heading your way at an unbelievable speed and swallowing everything in its path. Trees and buildings burst into flames as the ash passes over them.

Turn the page.

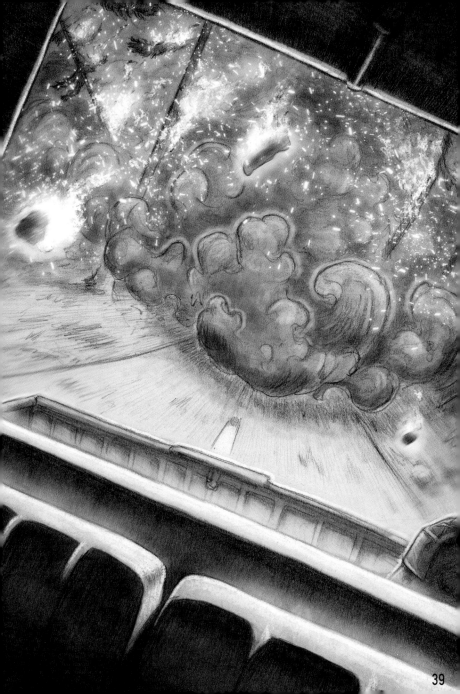

Frank curses as he drives, and the speed causes the truck to swerve wildly. You aren't sure what you're more afraid of—crashing into a tree or the cloud of ash that is on your heels.

The next time you dare to look back, the cloud of burning ash is right behind the pickup. You see Terry's eyes go wide in fear as you both realize it is hopeless. There is no way you can outrun the danger.

An intense wave of heat washes over you, and the truck is swallowed by the ash. Then your world goes black.

THE END

To follow another path, turn to page 10.
To learn more about supervolcanoes, turn to page 103.

As you start toward the cabin, you hear the **thwump-thwump-thwump** of a helicopter overhead. You move to the middle of the road and start waving and yelling. "Help us. Here! Down here!"

By some miracle, the pilot spots you. He swoops down and lands nearby. You duck and run toward the helicopter as its blades whirl overhead and kick up dust.

"Come on. Hurry!" the pilot waves you over. "Get buckled in."

His face is scrunched up in panic. You can see your own fear in the reflection of his sunglasses.

As you and Terry climb into the helicopter, you glance back toward the newly erupting volcanic vent. A giant, fiery cloud of ash is rolling toward you at an alarming speed. Trees and buildings burst into flames the instant it washes over them.

Turn the page.

You and Terry buckle up, and then the helicopter shoots skyward. It doesn't look like the helicopter will be able to outrun the cloud of ash. But it is flying upward as well as forward, and it is able to rise above the fiery cloud. You are hit by a wave of heat, and the helicopter wobbles from the turbulence. The world below turns into an ocean of dark, roiling gray.

Once it's clear you've passed beyond the ash, the pilot leans over to yell something to you and Terry. All you can make out is, "—military base!"

The helicopter winds its way through the mountains. Eventually you see a cluster of buildings organized in neat rows.

Turn to page 58.

Along with your bus, cars, campers, and numerous other vehicles clog the road. Even though park officials have made it so all lanes are exiting the park, the going is slow. Minutes tick by but you barely move.

Every now and then, the ground rumbles. Earthquakes shake your bus and cause some of your classmates to panic. Sobs come from the back of the bus. Some students try to call their parents, but the reception in the mountains is spotty.

The earthquakes seem to be getting stronger and more numerous. Panic seems to grow with every quake. The other drivers start honking at each other and try to cut in line. Mr. Thwaites walks from student to student trying to keep everyone calm. But you aren't sure how much it is really helping.

By mid-morning, your bus rumbles through the park's south exit. You let out a sigh of relief, thinking all will be safe. You're out of the Yellowstone caldera and about to start putting some miles between you and the park. Even the quakes seem to be letting up. You sit back in your seat and relax.

"Do you think everyone will get out OK?" Terry asks, leaning over the back of your seat.

"Yeah, probably." You frown. "That line was really long, though."

Just then someone calls out from the back of the bus. "Look! Look!"

Her shouts are followed by a loud roar echoing through the mountains.

Everyone turns toward the back of the bus to see what's happening. A thick jet of hot gases and ash shoots thousands of feet into the air.

Turn the page.

You watch in horror as a cloud of ash, pushed by the southerly winds, rushes forward from the explosion. It's traveling incredibly fast, like a fiery tidal wave. You turn to tell the bus driver to drive faster, but before you can open your mouth, the cloud has reached you. The gray ash washes over the bus, its searing heat melting everything.

THE END

To follow another path, turn to page 10.
To learn more about supervolcanoes, turn to page 103.

Your bus bounces down the road. Most of the traffic is heading south, so you make good time.

Despite that, it is a scary ride. The earthquakes seem to be growing stronger and more numerous. Mr. Thwaites keeps looking back nervously, and your classmates stare out the windows wide-eyed as if they are expecting the world to end any second.

Just days before, you were excited to see the signs leading into the park. Now you are thankful when you spot the exit sign along the road. Everyone in the bus lets out a sigh of relief as you leave the park.

You sit back and relax in your seat as the bus rumbles on.

"Do you think Brad and Izzy left, too?" Terry asks from the seat in front of you.

"I hope so," you say.

Turn the page.

Sometime later, you hear a loud rumble echoing through the mountains.

"Look!" a boy in the back of the bus shouts.

Everyone turns to see a huge plume of ash shooting upward into the sky. It must be at least 10 miles high, you think. Then a shock wave hits the bus, nearly causing it to veer off the winding road. Bags, drink containers, and passengers are jolted out of their seats.

Shouts and sobs fill the bus. Some students are huddled down in their seats while others just stare out the windows.

In front of the bus, you hear the bus driver mumble, "If we had taken the south exit and been downwind of that ... " He mops his brow.

Turn the page.

As you watch the eruption, a wave of hot gases, fiery rock, and solidified lava spread out from the volcano, covering everything in a dark gray cloud. You're thankful that you left when you did to get far enough away from the park.

As you continue on, the sky darkens and you can hear and see thunder and lightning. Then it begins to rain. People are complaining of being hungry and needing to go to the bathroom. You can see a water tower in the distance. That must mean a town is nearby.

To stop in town, turn to page 62.
To keep going, turn to page 66.

Your bus heads east as you roll through the mountains along a winding highway. It isn't the only vehicle on the road. Traffic is heavy, so the going is slow. It takes you about an hour just to get out of the park, and then a couple more hours before you reach the nearest town.

The bus stops at a convenience store so the students can stock up on supplies and use the restroom. As you're standing outside waiting for everyone to finish up, you hear a loud explosion. It echoes over the mountains, and even at this distance you can feel the ground shake. You turn to see a plume of ash rising skyward from the direction of Yellowstone Park

"Whoa!" Terry exclaims. "It's a good thing we left when we did."

"I hope Izzy got out of the park safely," you say.

Turn the page.

"I thought it'd be bigger," one of your classmates scoffs. "It doesn't look very 'super.'"

"That's just one vent opening up," Mr. Thwaites says, walking up behind you. "The whole volcano hasn't blown—yet. If any more vents open, we'll have a disaster on our hands."

Volcanic ash begins to fall like snow. It quickly turns the skies gray as it drifts along the easterly winds. You worry about the visibility as the ash starts to fall faster. Will the bus driver be able to see well enough to find your way?

To seek cover in town, turn to page 67.
To keep driving, turn to page 70.

Your tour bus heads west out of the park. There is a lot of traffic, as other people are leaving the park as well, so the going is slow. But you reach the exit within an hour.

You watch as the mountains fill the scenery. You're quickly putting miles between you and the park.

"OK," Mr. Thwaites says, standing up at the front of the bus. "We'll be stopping in the next town so you can stock up on food and water. Then we will make arrangements to get everybody safely home." Disappointed sighs fill the bus.

You know it's for the best that you're leaving, but you're still disappointed. You didn't want your trip to end so early.

"Hey, at least we won't have to finish up our projects," Terry says, trying to cheer you up.

Sometime later, one of your classmates in the back of the bus shouts, "Hey, what's that?"

You turn to see a column of dark gray ash streaming straight up into the sky. It must be miles high.

"Yellowstone just erupted!" Terry yells.

The bus is filled with astonished shouts. "No way!" "Whoa!" "I can't believe it!" One kid even says, "This will be an awesome addition to my project!"

"It's a good thing we left when we did," you say to Terry.

Turn the page.

"Yeah, no kidding," your friend replies. He lowers his voice. "I've tried texting Izzy and Brad. Haven't heard anything back."

"I'm sure they're OK," you say, swallowing.

For the next hour or so, everyone watches out their windows as the cloud of ash grows larger. The volcano is shooting tons of rocks and debris miles into the air.

Then the bus rolls into the next town. One sign points toward the nearest convenience store. Another points to the local airport.

To keep going on the tour bus, turn to page 72.
To get on a plane, turn to page 74.

You touch down at a military base a couple hundred miles from the park.

"Come on," the pilot says, helping you and Terry out of the helicopter. "Let's get you inside."

You look around. The base seems deserted. The sky over half the base is clear. The other half, the half shadowed by mountains, is turning gray. The cloud of ash looks much larger than before, even this far away.

The pilot catches what you're looking at.

"Another vent opened up while we were in flight," he says. "Folks think the whole thing is going to blow soon."

"So it's a supervolcano?" you ask.

"Yeah," the pilot nods. "Looks that way." Then he stares you right in the eye. "Do not repeat that. We don't need people panicking."

You and Terry are too stunned to say anything as the pilot leads you into a hangar. Instead of planes, it is filled with rows and rows of cots. Many of them are filled with people.

"Go find yourselves a couple open spots," the pilot say. "I'll see if they have some food."

You sit down next to some folks who are huddled around a radio. Through the static, you catch a jumble of words.

" ... all air traffic has been grounded ... "

" ... a fourth vent has opened up ... "

" ... national state of emergency ... "

You try to rest and eat the meal that the pilot brought you, but you can't stop listening to the radio.

Then, later that day, an earthquake rattles the hangar.

"What was that?" Terry asks.

Turn the page.

The radio answers for you: " ... the caldera has collapsed. Yellowstone has turned into a supervolcano ... "

You go to look outside. It's shocking. The world has turned gray. Ash rains down on the base. The air is hard to breathe, and you go back inside.

You are lucky that you made it to safety before Yellowstone erupted. But you have no idea how long you'll be stuck at the military base or what happened to your classmates. Your phones stopped working hours ago. You just hope the base has enough supplies to support everyone. Otherwise you'll be in serious trouble.

THE END
To follow another path, turn to page 10.
To learn more about supervolcanoes, turn to page 103.

"Mr. Thwaites," you say, tapping your science teacher on the shoulder. "Everyone is tired and hungry. Can we stop?"

Mr. Thwaites looks back at the students on the bus. They look ragged and tired from the rushed departure. Some just look afraid. Many are trying to call parents on their cell phones, but the reception is spotty up in the mountains. He takes a moment to weigh the options.

"Yeah, I suppose," he says eventually. "We should be far enough away to be safe. And I should report to the school."

The bus pulls into a convenience store. Students stream off the bus. Some hit the bathrooms, others head for the snack aisles, and Mr. Thwaites asks the store's attendant if there's a phone he can use.

You are waiting with Terry just inside the door when the rain turns to snow. Only it's not fluffy white flakes that are falling. They're gray.

"That's ash," Terry says. You look around. The sky is much darker than it was just a couple minutes ago.

The bus driver rushes inside to find Mr. Thwaites. He tries to whisper, but you can hear him anyway. "I don't know if it's gonna be safe out in this," the driver says. "It's starting to come down pretty thick, and we won't have much visibility."

Mr. Thwaites looks out the window. You follow his gaze. With the amount of ash and rain falling, you can barely make out the bus parked in the lot.

"OK, there's a motel across the way," Mr. Thwaites decides. "We can spend the night there."

Mr. Thwaites gathers up your classmates and leads them over to the motel. Luckily, there are still a couple rooms available. He gets one for the girls and one for the boys. It'll be crowded, but being surrounded by your classmates actually helps you feel more secure.

Turn the page.

With all that has happened, it's hard for anyone to fall asleep. A few are able to drift off, but you and Terry just stare out the window. There's not much to see. Ash has covered everything, turning the world dark gray. It's so thick you can barely see the streetlights.

Around midnight, you hear a creak above you.

"What's that?" Terry asks.

You look up at the ceiling. To your horror, a crack starts to form along the ceiling. As wood and plaster pop and snap, your classmates start to wake.

"Something's wrong," you say. "We need to ... "

Under the extreme weight of the ash, mixed with rain, the roof collapses, burying everyone.

THE END
To follow another path, turn to page 10.
To learn more about supervolcanoes, turn to page 103.

You tap on Mr. Thwaites' shoulder. "I don't think we should stop," you say. "We're still too close to the volcano." Mr. Thwaites nods in agreement and instructs the bus driver to keep going.

About half an hour outside of town, someone says, "Hey, it's snowing."

"That's not snow," Terry says.

You look out your window. What you see definitely aren't white puffy flakes. It's volcanic ash. The sky is turning a dark gray as it falls.

"We don't want to get stuck in this," the bus driver says, leaning back to talk to Mr. Thwaites. "The farther away we are, the better."

As the bus continues on, the driver turns up the radio. You hear reports about airports being closed and travel restrictions to the south and east. Winds are blowing most of the ash that way. Things could have been worse if you had left through a different exit.

To head north to Canada, turn to page 78.
To head west to the coast, turn to page 79.

Your group decides to spend the night in town. Mr. Thwaites checks you all into a motel. It's crowded in the two rooms, but you feel safer with a group.

After all the excitement of the day, you struggle to fall asleep. You're still awake around midnight when you hear a distant rumbling. You're not sure what it is, so you peek out the window. But it's too dark to see anything.

The next morning, as you open the door, you are shocked. Everything is covered in inches of ash. The air is thick with it, and you can hardly see 10 feet in front of you.

You learn from the motel manager that Yellowstone erupted overnight.

Mr. Thwaites tells everyone that they need to stay inside for their safety. Then the worst news comes. "The bus won't start," the bus driver says. "The engine's clogged with ash."

Turn the page.

"What are we going to do?" Mr. Thwaites asks.

The bus driver doesn't have an answer.

There is nothing you can do. The ash is suffocating. Every time someone tries to go outside, they start to hack and cough and are forced back inside.

The few bags of chips and bottles of water people were carrying with them quickly run out. The water from the faucet in your rooms turns dark gray after the first day. You have no supplies. You can't leave. You can't call for help. And you doubt any rescue worker could make it through the thick ash. When you develop a cough from breathing in the ashy air, you know it's the beginning of the end.

THE END

To follow another path, turn to page 10.
To learn more about supervolcanoes, turn to page 103.

"Everyone, quick! "Mr. Thwaites shouts. "We need to leave now!'

You and Terry go through the store to help him gather up your classmates.

"Come on, hurry up!" you shout. Some people leave immediately. Others grumble and slowly shuffle towards the exit.

"Come on! We don't want to get stuck here," your science teacher encourages everyone. "It's just going to get worse."

Soon you're back on the road. There is some grumbling from those who weren't able to get anything to eat. But as you look out the window, you understand Mr. Thwaites' concern. The ash is coming down thicker and thicker. They sky to the west of you is a dark gray, and all that ash is blowing your way. There's limited visibility, but the bus slowly keeps chugging on.

Some time in the middle of the night, the bus jerks to the side of the road, waking you. The bus driver curses as the bus' engine sputters and stalls.

"What's wrong?" you ask groggily.

"The ash has clogged the engine," the driver says, hitting the dashboard with his fist.

"Is there anything we can do?" Mr. Thwaites asks.

The bus driver just shakes his head. "We're not going anywhere."

"Well, we have hardly any water or food," Mr. Thwaites says. "We can't stay here."

You look out your window. All you can see is black. Ash has blocked out the moon and stars. Then you look back at your classmates. Most of them are asleep.

"Can we at least wait until morning?" you whisper. "We're all pretty tired."

Mr. Thwaites agrees. "But we'll have to figure out what to do then."

To seek cover, turn to page 91.
To keep going on foot, turn to page 95.

The bus pulls up to a convenience store. Students rush out. Some hit the bathrooms, while others go buy snacks.

You wait near the front door with Mr. Thwaites. You watch the ash cloud in the distance swirl with the wind. While most of it drifts to the east of you, some spreads out in your direction as well. It is slowly filling up the sky.

"Wow," you say. " I can't believe how big that ash cloud is."

"It's why we can't fly home," Mr. Thwaites says.

As if on cue, a light dusting of ash begins to fall. You hold out your hand to catch some of it in your palm.

"Really?" you say. "It doesn't look like much."

"Well, it's not really dust," Mr. Thwaites explains. "It's made up of tiny pieces of rock that could clog and destroy an engine, especially an airplane's."

Turn to page 79.

You find the airport, and Mr. Thwaites makes arrangements for you and your classmates to catch a plane to the nearest major hub. From there, you will be able to fly home.

As the plane prepares for takeoff, you sit back in your seat and stare out the window. In the distance, you see the ash cloud growing ever larger. Most of the debris blows east, carried by the winds. But some of it is slowly drifts in your direction, as the cloud of ash dominates the sky. You even notice small gray flakes starting to fall.

Then it is time for takeoff. You watch the ground drop away.

As the plane rises, the sky turns from blue to gray. The ash seems thicker the higher you go. You even see lightning flashes in the middle of the ash cloud.

The airplane banks, heading in the direction of the nearest major airport.

A short while later you hear an odd whining noise from outside. You look out your window to see smoke coming from one of the engines. With a loud pop, the engine bursts into flames.

Turn the page.

The ding of the "fasten seatbelt" light is strange to hear in the midst of disaster. The voice of the pilot blares over the speakers. "We have just lost an engine due to the volcanic ash," the pilot says. "We will need to make an emergency landing."

You look out your window. All you can see are mountains below. **Where are we?** you wonder.

The engine on the other side of the plane catches fire. The plane's previously slow descent rapidly increases. With both engines gone, there's nothing the pilot can do. The plane bursts into a ball of flame as it crashes into the side of a mountain.

THE END

To follow another path, turn to page 10.
To learn more about supervolcanoes, turn to page 103.

You convince Mr. Thwaites and the bus driver to keep heading north. They agree as the news reports on the radio say that everything south of you is being covered in ash.

Sometime after dinner, you reach the Canadian border. To your surprise, cars are backed up for miles. You aren't the only ones who had the idea to head north. But even though you and your classmates have your passports, no one is being allowed into the country.

You learn that Canadian officials have closed their borders to stop the stream of refugees. Instead they've set up camps. With no means of getting home, you and your classmates have no other choice. You find a couple unoccupied tents and settle down to wait.

The camp quickly fills up with people fleeing for safety. They tell you that the volcano is still spewing ash into the air. You're not sure when you'll be able to leave. But at least you're a safe distance from Yellowstone.

THE END
To follow another path, turn to page 10.
To learn more about supervolcanoes, turn to page 103.

Your group decides to head west, away from the volcano's fallout. It's night by the time you hit a major city. When you reach the edge of the city, traffic grinds to a stop. Cars are stalled on the sides of the road. Lines at the gas stations are blocks long. Employees hold signs that say, "Out of gas." A light dusting of ash fills the air.

"We're low on gas," the bus driver tells Mr. Thwaites. "We won't make it much farther. I don't even know if we can make it to a gas station, with how busy they are."

"We don't have much food or water, either," Mr. Thwaites says. "It's time to make a decision."

To stay in town, turn to page 80.
To keep driving, turn to page 84.

To preserve gas, the bus driver pulls over near a grocery store. Everyone pitches in what little money they have in their pockets and you run in.

The grocery store is crowded. You are surprised at how empty the shelves are already, but you manage to get some bottled water and enough food for everyone. Then you hunker down in the bus with your classmates.

As night encroaches, your surroundings darken. So do people's moods. Many travelers have been stranded for hours and are angry that they can't get gas. Others are upset that the grocery stores have run out of food.

Soon people begin yelling and screaming in the streets. As tempers flare, fights break out. Somewhere outside, glass shatters. An angry mob of people begins marching down the street. When they reach your bus, they start slamming their fists on its sides. You hear people chanting, "Food! Food! Food!"

Suddenly, the doors burst open. A half-dozen people storm onto the bus. Mr. Thwaites goes to block them, but he is pushed back down into his seat.

"It's just a bunch of kids," one of the rioters says.

"But they got food," another says, pointing to a box of cereal lying in the aisle.

"OK, pass what food you have up to us, and we'll leave you alone," the first rioter barks.

Turn the page.

Your classmates do as you're told.

In the coming days, things only grow worse. There are too many stalled cars on the road for your bus to leave. Even if you could leave, you wouldn't get very far.

To make matters worse, ash continues to fall, making it difficult to breathe. Rioters continue to fill the streets. It's dangerous to even be outside.

Now all you can do is hunker down in the bus and wait. You hope that rescue workers reach you before you starve or the rioters attack again.

THE END

To follow another path, turn to page 10.
To learn more about supervolcanoes, turn to page 103.

The bus driver keeps winding his way through the city. The traffic is thick, and there are many stalled cars. The people who have gotten out to walk make it difficult too. The going is slow.

You can see that people are frustrated and angry. There is shouting. Fights break out. You are thankful that you didn't stop. The streets look dangerous.

A couple hours outside of town, the bus runs out of gas. You're too far from the city to think of turning back. It didn't seem safe to stop for gas before. So you and your classmates pack up the little food and water you have and keep heading west on foot.

Cars pass you, but no one stops. A light dusting of ash begins to fall. People choke and cough. You pull a spare T-shirt from your backpack and tear off a strip to tie over your nose and mouth.

"Here," you say to Terry. "This will help."

You hand your friends the rest of your T-shirt. Your classmates copy you.

You keep trudging along. The highway is littered with stalled cars and angry people.

To keep to the main road, turn to page 86.
To take a side road, turn to page 89.

You decide to stay on the main road, despite the growing crowds of people. As you walk, your group grows. Your small group of students easily doubles and then triples in size.

As you continue on, you cross paths with a convoy of military trucks. They stop, and soldiers jump out to pass around bottles of water.

"Everyone, this way," a soldier toward the back of the line shouts. You and your classmates line up and then get into one of the trucks. "We've set up a shelter about an hour down the road," he says, pointing. "We have food and water there."

The shelter is in a high school. You're led to the gym where cots have been set up. The smell of food drifts in from the cafeteria, and you feel your stomach rumble from hunger.

In the coming days, the people at the shelter take good care of you. Having food, water, and rest is a huge relief.

Turn the page.

You spend your days inside. A light coat of ash has fallen across the town, and you've all been warned about the dangers of breathing it in. Not only can it cause you to choke and cough, but it may lead to serious lung illnesses.

You spend most of your time listening to the radio. What you hear saddens you. For hundreds of miles around Yellowstone, a thick layer of ash has covered everything. Thousands of people are believed to be dead, and millions are struggling to survive.

You are thankful to have reached safety, yet you have no idea when you will be able to return home and see your family again.

THE END

To follow another path, turn to page 10.
To learn more about supervolcanoes, turn to page 103.

You worry about the growing crowds of people traveling along the road. They are hungry and frustrated. Some of the more aggressive people have started to pick fights with one another. You suggest to Mr. Thwaites that your group head off down a side road.

"I saw a sign for a town that way," you say.

"We could use some food and water," Mr. Thwaites admits. Your group turns off from the main highway.

A couple miles later, you come across a stalled-out van. A woman and her husband are huddled over a flat tire, trying to fix it.

"Can we help?" you ask.

The couple accepts your offer, and you and Terry are able to change the tire for them.

Afterward, the woman asks, "Would you like a ride into town?"

"We couldn't take you all in one trip," the man adds. "But we could come back for the rest."

Turn the page.

It's a generous offer, and you take it. Once in the town, you are surprised at how different it is from the city. People are worried and scared about what's happening at Yellowstone. But no one's rioting or fighting. Few, if any, people drive through town, so there is still plenty of food on the grocery store shelves.

It's not home, but until the volcano stops venting ash into the air, which could be days from now, you won't be able to travel home safely. And even after that, you aren't sure how you'll get home. But at least for now you have a comfortable place to stay.

THE END

To follow another path, turn to page 10.
To learn more about supervolcanoes, turn to page 103.

You wake as Mr. Thwaites and the bus driver are making plans to find shelter. They try to whisper, but you and Terry overhear anyway.

"I thought I saw a convenience store about a mile back," Terry interrupts.

Neither of the adults want to walk back the way you came. "It's better than not knowing where we're going in all this ash," you point out.

Mr. Thwaites and the bus driver look out the window. Outside, the ash is still falling, turning the world, the ground, the sky, trees, and cars gray.

"OK everyone," Mr. Thwaites says, standing up at the front of the bus. "We are going to seek shelter. There's a convenience store about a mile back." Excited whispers pass through the bus. Most of them haven't had much to eat since you left the park.

Turn the page.

"But before we head out," Mr. Thwaites says, "we'll all need to protect ourselves from the ash. It will make you choke and cough, and even make you sick."

Everyone starts pulling out extra T-shirts from their bags and ripping them into strips that they tie over their faces. Once everyone is set, you head out.

The going is rough. A couple inches of ash cover the ground. Walking only kicks it up, causing people to cough and hack. And more ash is falling. Ash is in your nose, eyes, mouth, and ears. But you know you have to keep going.

It probably takes you an hour to walk the mile back to the store. When you get there, you are welcomed inside. There are about 20 other people there, most of whom had been stranded like you. The owners of the store have kindly welcomed everyone.

"We have enough food and water for a couple weeks," the owner says.

Turn the page.

You are thankful for that. The volcano does not stop erupting and throwing up ash for days. Every day more people show up. Just as you worry the store is about to run out of food, rescue workers arrive.

Everyone is taken by military truck to a shelter several hours away. You feel confident that you'll be safe and well cared for. But once there, no one can answer you when you ask, "How long before we can go home?" Ash has fallen hundreds and thousands of miles from Yellowstone. Air traffic is limited and most cars can't make it through the ash-covered landscape. You'll just have to wait it out.

THE END

To follow another path, turn to page 10.
To learn more about supervolcanoes, turn to page 103.

The next morning, you hear the bus driver and Mr. Thwaites talking.

" … we have no other choice," the bus driver says.

"Then it's settled," Mr. Thwaites says. "We head out on foot."

"What about the ash?" you ask.

"If we don't leave now, it could completely cover us," Mr. Thwaites says. "We have no way of knowing when it will end." He stands near the front of the bus to get everyone's' attention. "OK everyone, pack up. We're going to keep going on foot. We aren't sure when rescue workers might reach us, and this ash is preventing us from driving anywhere."

As you look outside, you realize that it is eerily quiet. Even though you're on a major highway, there is no traffic whatsoever.

Turn the page.

"But first, we need to protect ourselves from the ash," Mr. Thwaites explains. "Breathing it in can be dangerous. Please, cover you noses and mouths." Everyone starts to pull spare T-shirts from their bags. They rip them up into strips, and then tie the strips over their faces.

"But what if we do breathe it in?" someone asks.

"If we're not out in it for too long, it should be OK," Mr. Thwaites says.

The going is rough. Several inches of ash lay on the ground. You kick it up as you walk. Your nose starts to run, and you see Terry's eyes are getting red. One of your classmates with asthma begins to cough. And the ash keeps falling. The only reason people don't complain is because talking would mean breathing in more of the ash.

About midday, you come to a turnoff in the road. One sign points to a town 10 miles away, off the main highway. A second sign directs you to another town about 7 miles away, down a side road.

To stay on the main highway, turn to page 98.
To take the side road, turn to page 100.

"Shouldn't we stay on the main road?" you say.

"You're right," Mr. Thwaites says. "The highway is better marked than the side road. And we wouldn't want to get lost out here. And if anyone comes to help, there's a better chance it'll be on this road."

Even though several people in your group complain about the extra distance, you stick to the highway.

A couple hours later, you are rewarded when a convoy of military trucks stops for you. Soldiers jump out and pass bottles of water around. Then you are all led into the back of a truck. From there, you are driven to a shelter.

While the shelter isn't home, at least you're out of the ash. No one can say how long you will be there, as the volcano hasn't stopped erupting. But for now, you are safe.

THE END
To follow another path, turn to page 10.
To learn more about supervolcanoes, turn to page 103.

Mr. Thwaites and the bus driver discuss staying on the main road.

"It's much shorter if we take the side road," you object. In the ash, 3 miles is a huge difference.

"And we're almost out of water," Terry adds. "We need to get somewhere quick."

"OK, OK," Mr. Thwaites says. "Let's head that way then."

About an hour after the turn off, though, you begin to wonder if you made the right choice. With inches of ash already on the ground, and more falling every minute, it's hard to tell where you're going. The road isn't very well marked, and you are surrounded by grayness. Gray ground, gray sky. Even your classmates' faces are gray.

"I think we're lost," Terry chokes.

You think your friend might be right.

"Are we even on the road?" someone asks.

You check by kicking at the dust and are horrified to dig up dirt and weeds. You think you're in a field of some sort.

And what's worse, the ash fall is worsening and getting thicker. People in your group are coughing and hacking more.

"Come on," you yell. "We have to keep going."

But it's hopeless. You try to follow your footsteps back to the road, but between the falling ash and blowing wind, you quickly lose them. Then people start having extreme difficulties breathing because of the ash that they've sucked into their lungs.

You don't last much longer before you collapse to the ground, unable to breathe.

THE END
To follow another path, turn to page 10.
To learn more about supervolcanoes, turn to page 103.

AFTERMATH

The likelihood that a volcano, let alone a supervolcano, will erupt again around the Yellowstone caldera is extremely rare. The last volcanic eruption occurred about 174,000 years ago, and the last "super" volcano, which created the caldera, happened more than 600,000 years ago. But the Yellowstone volcano is still considered active because of all the earthquakes that occur in and around the park—between 1,000 and 3,000 earthquakes shake Yellowstone every year. It also has thermal features, including hot springs, thermal vents, and geysers.

Yellowstone is just one of a handful of active supervolcanoes in the world. Several are in Asia. But the Long Valley caldera in California and the Valle Grande caldera in New Mexico are located in the United States. Like Yellowstone they suffer numerous small earthquakes every year. They also have thermal features, like hot springs and steam vents.

But the earthquake activity around these calderas isn't as great as at Yellowstone, and they don't have nearly as many thermal features. Some people worry Yellowstone could be the next supervolcano to erupt.

A supervolcano eruption would be comparable to a small asteroid striking Earth or hundreds of nuclear bombs exploding all in one spot. Everything near the eruption will be destroyed. That destruction would spread out for hundreds of miles around the volcano as clouds of gases and ash, called pyroclastic flows, race outward from the eruption. This ash is heated to hundreds of degrees, and anyone caught in its path will die instantly. Around the globe, 200 million people live within a volcano's danger zone.

Volcanoes also shoot ash miles into the air. A supervolcano would send up thousands of tons of ash. Winds would carry this ash around the globe, stopping most air traffic for weeks. Any planes caught in the air around the blast could crash as the ash clogs up their engines.

The ash would fall like snow hundreds, even thousands, of miles away. It will be dangerous to be outside, as it will be difficult to breathe or even see. Travel will come to a standstill. Plants and animals in the path of the volcanic ash will die. Water will be polluted, and a national food shortage is likely.

Those are just some of the short-term effects. Long term, a supervolcano eruption would change Earth's climate. After all, a massive volcanic eruption is one theory behind the extinction of the dinosaurs. All that ash floating around in the sky will block out the sun's rays, causing temperatures to drop. The cold spell could last for years, further worsening food shortages as farmers struggle to grow their crops.

Millions of lives could be lost. Billions of dollars would be spent on cleanup. It would take years for the temperatures to get back to normal, and up to 10 years for the land around the volcano to recover enough to support life. Not a person on the planet would go unaffected by a supervolcano eruption.

TEN TIPS ON HOW TO SURVIVE A SUPERVOLCANO

- **Just because a volcano is considered active, like the Yellowstone caldera, does not mean there's danger of an eruption.** It just means that a future eruption is possible. And while volcanoes tend to be unpredictable, scientists do have the means to monitor activity. Events such as earthquakes and CO_2 gases venting are signs of a potential eruption. Pay attention to these signs whenever you're near an active volcano. Most often, there will enough of a warning to get safely away before a volcano erupts.

- **Get away from an erupting volcano as quickly as you can**. A supervolcano could incinerate everything within a 100-mile radius. You won't be safe even if you find shelter in a sturdy building. The falling ash alone would spread out for hundreds of miles. So the farther you are away, the better your chances of survival.

- **Do not travel downwind of an erupting volcano.** That is the direction the volcanic ash will most likely travel. Get out of the path of the falling ash.

- **Avoid air travel around an erupting volcano.**
  Volcanic ash is made up of tiny rocks. The rocks
  can and will wreck the engines of most vehicles.
  A supervolcano could kick up so much ash that it
  prevents air travel worldwide.

- **Avoid breathing in volcanic ash.** When mixed
  with the moisture in your lungs, it turns into a
  cementlike consistency, making it very difficult
  to breathe. Breathing in the ash may also lead to
  lung diseases.

- **When ash is falling, do not seek shelter in
  buildings with flat roofs.** The weight of the
  ash, especially if mixed with rain, will cause the roof
  to collapse.

- **Always travel away from an erupting volcano.**
  If a supervolcano eruption does occur, it could last for
  days and disrupt travel for weeks. Emergency workers
  will not be able to reach people right away, especially
  those nearest the volcano. It might be best if you can
  get to them.

- **Stay away from steep slopes and the banks of rivers.** Volcanic ash can build up on the sides of mountains and canyons. If mixed with water, snow, or ice, the ash can create swift-moving mudflows known as lahars.

- **If you're traveling, stay on major roads.** Falling ash will obscure your surroundings and could cause you to get lost. Also, rescue vehicles are more likely to use major roads, which would increase the chances of you being found.

- **Bring along a survival kit** whenever traveling to a remote place, especially if there is the potential of danger.

SURVIVAL KIT

*flint stone for making fire (waterproof matches will work also, but there will also be a limited amount)

*iodine tablets for making water drinkable

*utility knife

*first-aid kit

*fishing kit, with line, hooks, and sinkers

*nylon rope, at least 25 feet

*compass and map of the local area

*tarp, to use for shelter

*whistle, to use as an alarm in case of danger

*Mylar blanket, for warmth

*poncho, gloves, and stocking cap

*duct tape, for repairs

*plastic bags, for storage

*cooking pots and eating utensils

*hand-crank radio

*flashlights, with spare batteries

*walkie-talkies, with spare batteries

*extra set of warm clothes, jacket, and hiking shoes

*stainless steel water bottle

*bottled water (as much as you can carry)

* non-perishable food (snack bars, jerky, instant soup, and cereal)

GLOSSARY

AFTERSHOCK (AF-tur-shok)—a small earthquake that follows a large one

ASH (ASH)—a powder that results from an explosion; ash comes out of a volcano when it erupts

CALDERA (kal-DAYR-uh)—a collapsed volcano

EVACUATE (i-VA-kyuh-wayt)—to leave a dangerous place to go somewhere safer

GEYSER (GYE-zur)—an underground spring that shoots hot water and steam through a hole in the ground

HARMONIC TREMOR (har-MON-ik TREM-uhr)—a continued release of seismic energy, usually caused by the movement of underground magma

INCINERATE (in-SIN-uh-rayt)—to destroy by burning

MAGMA (MAG-muh)—melted rock found beneath Earth's surface

OBSERVATORY (uhb-ZUR-vuh-tor-ee)—buildings designed to study something; the Yellowstone Volcano Observatory studies volcanoes and earthquakes in Yellowstone National Park

PLATEAU (pla-TOH)—an area of high, flat land

RICHTER SCALE (RIK-tur SKALE)—a scale that measures the amount of energy in an earthquake; earthquakes with low numbers cause little or no damage

SEISMIC (SIZE-mik)—something that is caused by an earthquake

THERMAL FEATURE (THUR-muhl FEE-chur)—a hole in the Earth's crust that lets hot water, steam, vapors, and gases escape; geysers and hot springs are thermal features

VENT (VENT)—a hole in a volcano; hot ash, steam, and lava blow out of vents from an erupting volcano

READ MORE

Furgang, Kathy. *Everything Volcanoes & Earthquakes.* Washington, D.C.: National Geographic, 2013.

Gilbert, Sara. *Yellowstone.* Mankato, Minn.: Creative Education, 2016.

Katirgis, Jane, and Michele Ingber Drohan. *Volatile Volcanoes.* New York: Enslow Publishing, 2015.

Royston, Angela. *The Science of Volcanoes.* New York: Gareth Stevens Publishing, 2013.

INTERNET SITES

Use FactHound to find Internet sites related to this book.
All of the sites on FactHound have been researched by our staff.

Here's all you do:
Visit *www.facthound.com*
Type in this code: 9781491481080

AUTHOR

Blake Hoena wrote his first story in second grade. It was about space aliens trying to steal the moon. And ever since, he has been fascinated with little green men. He even created a graphic novel series about alien brothers, Eek and Ack, who try to conquer our big blue home. When not thinking about outer space, Blake writes children's books about mythology, skateboarding, and poetry. He lives in St. Paul, Minnesota, with his wife, two kids, and a couple of pets.

ILLUSTRATOR

Filippo Vanzo was born in Vicenza, Italy. His art is a blend of both traditional and digital media, often using pencil or ink drawings colored digitally. Nature in all its forms is also a strong source of inspiration.

Filippo loves nature, hiking, maps, dinosaurs, video games, progressive and folk music, riding his bicycle, and sleeping. If he were not an illustrator, he would probably want be a wildlife photographer, a natural reserve ranger, a paleontologist, or a tree.